W9-BEK-695

21st Century Junior Library

Scorpion

by Katie Marsico

CHERRY LAKE PUBLISHING * ANN ARBOR, MICHIGAN

Published in the United States of America by Cherry Lake Publishing
Ann Arbor, Michigan
www.cherrylakepublishing.com

Content Adviser: The Entomological Foundation (www.entfdn.org)

Reading Adviser: Marla Conn, ReadAbility, Inc

Photo Credits: © Mauro Rodrigues/Shutterstock Images, cover; © efendy/Shutterstock Images, 4;
© Sebastian Janicki/Shutterstock Images, 6; © Sainam51/Shutterstock Images, 8; © Arto Hakola/
Shutterstock Images, 10; © blackeagleEMJ/Shutterstock Images, 12; © KobchaiMa/Shutterstock
Images, 14; © reptiles4all/Shutterstock Images, 16; © Braam Collins/Shutterstock Images, 18;
© Mr. SUTTIFON YAKHAM/Shutterstock Images, 20

LIBRARY OF CONGRESS CATALOGING-IN-PUBLICATION DATA
Marsico, Katie, 1980- author.
  Scorpion / by Katie Marsico.
      pages cm —(Creepy crawly critters)
  Includes bibliographical references and index.
  ISBN 978-1-63362-594-5 (hardcover)—ISBN 978-1-63362-684-3 (pbk.) —
ISBN 978-1-63362-774-1 (pdf)—ISBN 978-1-63362-864-9 (ebook)
  1. Scorpion—Juvenile literature. I. Title. II. Series: Creepy crawly critters.

QL458.7.M36 2015
595.4'6—dc23   2015005835

---

*Cherry Lake Publishing would like to acknowledge the work of
the Partnership for 21st Century Skills.
Please visit www.p21.org for more information.*

Printed in the United States of America
Corporate Graphics

CONTENTS

Scorpions are known to sting.

Little Stinging Lobsters?

Have you ever seen a scorpion up close? It looks like a miniature lobster, except that it lives on land. Scorpions are famous for their **venomous** sting. What else makes them unique? Let's find out more about scorpions!

The tip of a scorpion's tail is venomous.

Let's Study a Scorpion's Body!

Scorpions are **arachnids**. This **class** of animals also includes mites, spiders, and ticks. An arachnid has two main body segments and eight legs. A scorpion's front pair of legs features powerful claws, or pincers. Its tail ends in a venomous tip called a **telson**.

7

Some birds, like this kingfisher from Thailand, catch and eat scorpions.

Scorpions use their pincers and telson to defend themselves against **predators**. Bats, birds, mice, rats, lizards, and snakes all hunt scorpions for food. Scorpions sometimes even attack and eat each other! Mainly they feed on insects and spiders. Mice and lizards serve as food for a few larger scorpions.

This scorpion has caught some prey.

Scorpions rely on their pincers and telson to hunt, too. A scorpion lashes its tail at a person or animal to deliver a powerful sting. The venom in its telson can **paralyze** or kill **prey**. Other times they crush their prey without any venom.

Make a Guess!

Scorpions have a pair of fanglike mouthparts called chelicerae. The sharp chelicerae help pull apart and mash up meat. Scorpions are only able to eat food in liquid form. Can you guess why they need chelicerae?

Some scorpions live in wooded areas.

Habitats and Habits

Scorpions have existed on Earth for hundreds of millions of years. There are currently about 2,000 **species** of these arachnids. They are found on every continent except Antarctica. Scorpions often live in deserts and grasslands. Yet some species also spend time in forest and mountain **habitats**.

Scorpions often hide in safe places,
like under some leaves.

Scorpions are **nocturnal**. They are sensitive to light, so they are most active at night. During daytime hours, scorpions usually hide. A few spend time in trees and bushes. Most burrow, or dig holes, in rock piles, soil, or sand. This is why most scorpions prefer areas where **frost** never coats the ground.

Baby scorpions, called scorplings, ride
on their mother's back.

In the wild, most scorpions live for three to eight years. Unlike many arachnids, female scorpions do not lay eggs. Instead, scorpions give birth to babies called scorplings. The mother often carries the scorplings on her back until they're a few weeks old.

Look!

Look at the scorplings in this photo. Then look at the mother scorpion the babies are riding on. What similarities do you notice? How about differences? The appearance of the scorplings will change as they molt, or shed their skin.

Some people keep scorpions as pets,
but they can be dangerous.

Living Alongside People

Some people keep scorpions as pets. Still, many humans dislike them. This is especially true in areas where scorpions live near homes and businesses. People fear a scorpion's venomous sting. Yet different species produce different types of venom. Only 25 to 30 species of scorpions have a sting that is dangerous to people.

If you live in an area with scorpions around, be careful when you walk outside.

Luckily, a little extra **caution** helps humans stay safe. For example, it's important to be careful when playing near rock piles where scorpions hide.

These arachnids are amazing animals. By learning more about them, people often end up more fascinated than afraid!

Ask Questions!

Think about what else you'd like to learn about scorpions. For instance, are you curious about what species live in your area? Just ask an arachnologist! That's a scientist who studies scorpions and other arachnids.

GLOSSARY

arachnids (uh-RAK-nuhdz) animals that lack a backbone and antennae and have two main body segments and four pairs of legs

caution (KAW-shuhn) effort to avoid danger

class (KLASS) a category of animals that are grouped together according to features they share

frost (FRAWST) a thin layer of ice that forms on the ground when the air becomes cold

habitats (HAB-ih-tatz) places where an animal or plant normally lives and grows

nocturnal (nahk-TUR-nuhl) mainly active at night

paralyze (PAR-uh-lize-ez) make something unable to move

predators (PRED-uh-turz) animals that kill other animals for food

prey (PRAY) animals that are killed by other animals for food

species (SPEE-sheez) one type, or kind, of plant or animal

telson (TEL-suhn) the tip of a scorpion's tail

venomous (VEH-nuh-muhss) full of a naturally produced substance that acts much like a poison

FIND OUT MORE

BOOKS

Franchino, Vicky. *Scorpions.*
New York: Children's Press, 2015.

Lynette, Rachel. *Scorpions.*
New York: PowerKids Press, 2013.

Pringle, Laurence, and Meryl
Henderson (illustrator). *Scorpions!
Strange and Wonderful.* Honesdale,
PA: Boyds Mills Press, 2013.

WEB SITES

National Geographic Kids—Scorpion

*http://kids.nationalgeographic
.com/animals/scorpion/*
Check out additional fascinating
facts about scorpions and
their relatives.

San Diego Zoo Kids—Scorpion

*http://kids.sandiegozoo.org
/animals/arthropods/scorpion*
Learn more about scorpions and
browse several interesting photos
of them!

INDEX

ABOUT THE AUTHOR

Katie Marsico is the author of more than 200 children's books. She lives in a suburb of Chicago, Illinois, with her husband and children. Ms. Marsico would like to dedicate this book to Ms. Schwerdtmann and her class at Edison School.